The Power OF WELCOME

REAL-LIFE REFUGEE AND MIGRANT JOURNEYS

SCHOLASTIC

CONTENTS

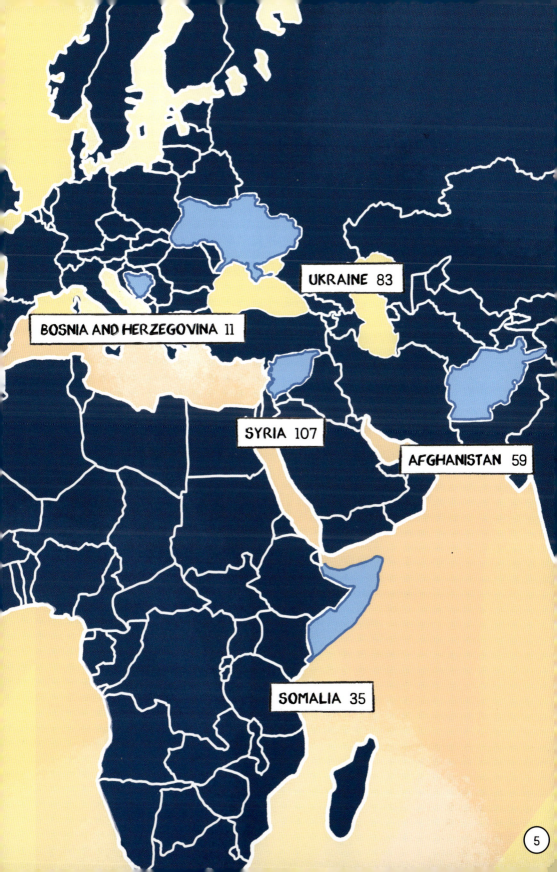

UKRAINE 83

BOSNIA AND HERZEGOVINA 11

SYRIA 107

AFGHANISTAN 59

SOMALIA 35

THE
OF W
BOS
& HERZI

WRITTEN AND ILLUSTRATED
BY ADA JUSIC

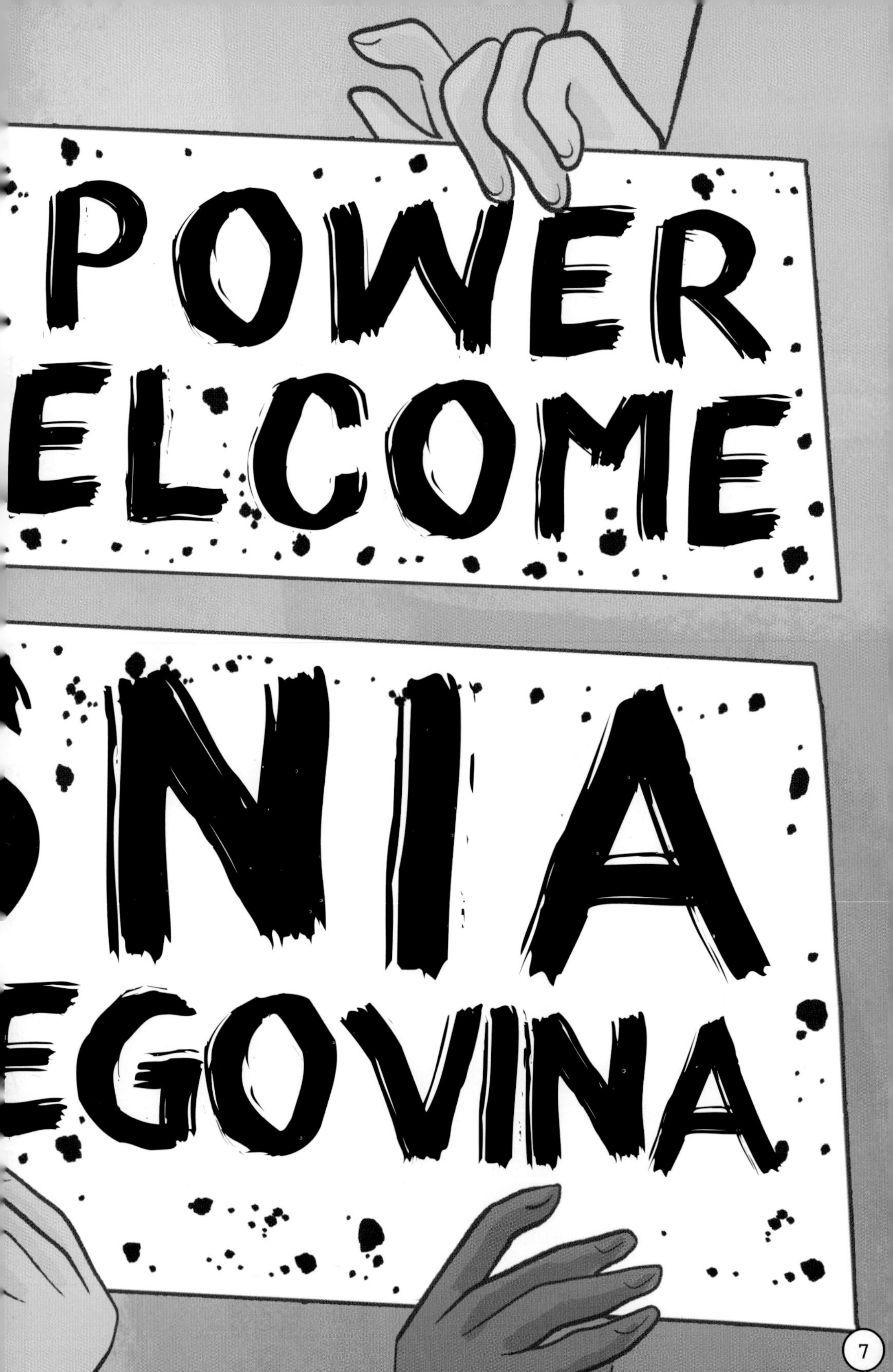
POWER
ELCOME
NIA
EGOVINA

BOSNIA AND HERZEGOVINA is a mountainous country in southeastern Europe. The area is known as the Balkans. Bosnia's history is complicated and it has been ruled by many different groups of people. In 9 CE, the Romans conquered the land for their empire. During this time, it was part of a province called Dalmatia. When the Roman Empire split into two (in 395 CE), the area became part of the Western Roman Empire. The Byzantine Empire (from modern-day Turkey) went on to conquer and rule Bosnia. The Byzantines were mostly Christians, and Christianity spread across the region.

The Byzantine Empire came into conflict with different tribes in the Balkans, such as the Ostrogoths and the Huns. The Huns were a tribe from central and southeastern Europe. They were led by a ruler, Attila, and created their

own empire. The Hun Empire collapsed after Attila died. The Ostrogoths also came from Europe, and created a Gothic empire. They fought the Byzantines for control of Bosnia but the Byzantine Empire won.

In the sixth century, a group of people called Slavs arrived and settled and ruled over large parts of Bosnia. Empires fought each other for control of land. Parts of Bosnia fell to Hungary, some were ruled by Serbs and some by Croats.

By the fourteenth century, Bosnia was a powerful and independent state. But this would change quickly. Within a hundred years, an empire from the East conquered Bosnia. The Ottoman Empire had taken over many Byzantine territories. The Ottoman's power was based in Constantinople (now Istanbul) and they were Turks. The Ottomans were Muslims, and their religion spread across Bosnia. In 1877–78, the Ottomans lost Bosnia to Russia and the Serbs after a short war.

The Russians gave up Bosnia during peace talks after the war. Bosnia was now controlled by the Austro-Hungarian empire. In 1908, the empire took over Bosnia entirely. Many Bosnians began to call for independence and conflict between the different religious groups grew. It remained this way until the end of World War One (1914–1918). The war started when

Archduke Franz Ferdinand, the heir to the Austro-Hungarian Empire, was assassinated by a man called Gavrilo Princip. The war caused the Austro-Hungarian Empire to fall.

Bosnia and Herzegovina were now part of the Kingdom of Serbs, Croats and Slovenes. In 1929, the country was renamed Yugoslavia. The largest ethnic groups in Yugoslavia were the Bosnians, the Serbs and the Croats.

After World War Two began in 1939, Germany and their allies invaded Yugoslavia in 1941. The National Socialist German Workers' Party, later known as Nazis, were anti-Semitic (anti-Jewish) and ruled Germany during this time. The region was soon overwhelmed and Yugoslavia was dismantled and Croatia, and parts of Bosnia, became a Nazi state (they were now ruled by the Nazis), and violence between the groups was common.

After the war ended, Yugoslavia became an independent republic (a republic doesn't have a monarchy and is ruled by an elected head of state) under the rule of Josep Tito. Tito had led the largest resistance to the Nazis during the war – the Partisans. With Tito as Yugoslavia's ruler, the former kingdom was replaced by a federation

of six equal republics with elected officials: Croatia, Montenegro, Serbia, Bosnia and Herzegovina, Slovenia and Macedonia. At this time, the different ethnic and religous groups, such as Muslims and Catholics, lived alongside each other peacefully.

Yugoslavia became a communist state. Europe was divided between East and West. The East was allied with the USSR (Union of Soviet Social Republics or the Soviet Union for short), a communist state including Russia and other countries where wealth had to be shared between the people. Tito refused to join the Soviet Union, so Yugoslavia was still independent. After Tito's death in 1980, ethnic-nationalism began to rise in the country. This is a belief that people's identity should be defined by a shared heritage, which usually includes a common language, religion and ancestry. However this can lead to believing that people of other ethnicities are second-class or undesirable citizens.

By 1991, the Soviet Union had collapsed. Yugoslavia fell apart as the different regions asked for freedom. In 1992, Bosnia and Herzegovina declared independence. However, Bosnia's Serb population rejected their independence and seized Sarajevo, the capital city of Bosnia and Herzegovina. Bosnian Serbs began to persecute and attack Bosniaks (Muslims in Bosnia) in

Sarajevo and across Bosnia. The Bosnian-Serb forces shot and killed civilians, forcing thousands of Bosniaks to flee to the cities of Srebrenica and Žepa which were designated as 'Safe Areas' by the United Nations (UN). Set up in 1945, the UN brings countries together to prevent another conflict like the Second World War.

Many Bosniaks hoped to find safety in the 'Safe Areas', but Radovan Karadžić, the Bosnian-Serb's political leader, told his forces to target these areas too. On 2 July 1995, the Bosnian-Serb forces attacked Srebrenica and on 11 July, they entered the city to forcibly drive the Bosniaks out. From 13 to 19 July 1995, all Bosniaks that were found outside of Srebrenica were captured and executed. When the war ended in 1995, close to 100,000 Bosniaks had been killed and more than 2 million had been displaced.

Since the last war, Bosnia has been rebuilt. It is now an independent state. The three main groups share power, each having a president for eight months at a time. This nation has a total population of about 3.8 million people, most of whom speak either Bosnian, Croatian or Serbian, and many speak all three. Bosnia is a multi-ethnic, multicultural country, with a complicated history. From 1992 onwards, many Bosnian refugees fled the country and now live across Europe, from Sweden to Germany and elsewhere.

We're safe now.

Safe, because we came to live in England, hundreds of miles from the home we left behind. And the war.

Mum's taking a photo of us.

A photo to send in a letter to Sarajevo, where I'm from.

I miss my grandparents too.

BBC

WAR IN BOSNIA . . . .

Our dad is still there. I really miss him. I wish he could be with us, but Mum says he can't get here yet because of the war.

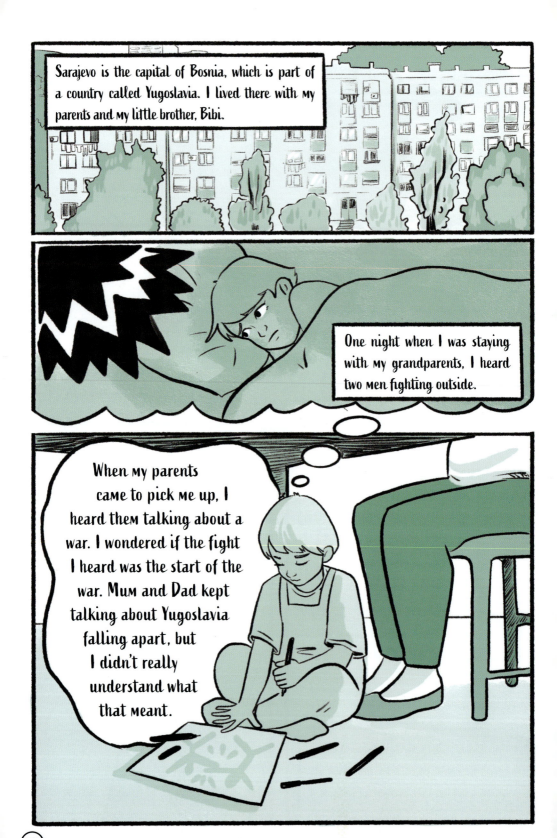

Sarajevo is the capital of Bosnia, which is part of a country called Yugoslavia. I lived there with my parents and my little brother, Bibi.

One night when I was staying with my grandparents, I heard two men fighting outside.

When my parents came to pick me up, I heard them talking about a war. I wondered if the fight I heard was the start of the war. Mum and Dad kept talking about Yugoslavia falling apart, but I didn't really understand what that meant.

Then everything started to change.

Mum look! Tanks!

There's so little food on the shelves....

Is ... is that a sniper?

The sounds of the guns, planes and the bombs were so loud, it was very scary.

When I watched cartoons with Grandpa he put his hands over my ears to try and block the sound out.

Then one day Mum took me to the local playground.

CRACK

CRACK!

CRACK!!

We couldn't stay in Bosnia anymore.

YUGOSLAVIA

My family was Muslim. In Bosnia, Muslims, Catholics and Orthodox Christians all lived peacefully together, but the Serbian politicians didn't like that. They thought Bosnia should be part of Serbia and that Muslims didn't belong there.

One day, Mum got a call from her cousin.

We need to be at the airport at 3p.m. There's a plane we can leave on.

Dad tried to call a taxi to take us to the airport.

No one will take us. They say it's too dangerous.

We don't have enough petrol in the car.

We don't have a choice.

SARAJEVO AIRPORT

No one stopped our car at any of the checkpoints until we got to the last one at the airport.

The soldiers wouldn't let Dad go with us.

"You're not on the list! Go away!"

"Are you going to shoot us?"

We'd had to say goodbye to Granny and Grandpa and now we had to say goodbye to Dad. How could we go without him?

"Be brave and look after Mum. I will be with you again soon."

We went inside the airport with Mum. Everyone was too afraid to speak.

We waited for hours and hours, with no food or water. We were so hungry and thirsty.

There was a sound like thunder.

BOOOOOOOM

A big plane, the biggest plane we'd ever seen, was landing! The sound made Bibi cry.

Stay here!

Can you take us on your plane?

I'm sorry, you're not on my list.

We waited again for hours.

Suddenly, everyone started walking out onto the runway. We followed them.

A little plane was on the runway. People were getting on.

At last!

We were on our way to England.

I watched everything and everyone I know disappear from the window.

↑✈ Arrivals

My aunty and uncle met us at the airport in England. They gave us all a big hug.

My uncle gave me a chocolate bar. I had never eaten chocolate before.

We live with them now. Mum, Bibi and I share a room.

Mum, when is Dad coming home?

I am very happy to live here with them but very sad that Dad isn't here with us.

Dad sends us letters back from Sarajevo. He writes about how much he misses us and that we have to be good and look after Mum for him. The letters take such a long time to arrive, sometimes months after he wrote them.

Mum worries about him a lot.

Mum, is Dad there?

My aunty has a neighbour called Gordana.

Gordana is Serbian but she isn't like the politicians or the soldiers, she's very nice and friendly.

Gordana is an artist.

I think I would like to be an artist.

I don't speak English, so when I start school, it is very confusing.

But the teachers are friendly and kind, even if I don't understand everything.

And I am starting to make friends.

One day, Mum comes to pick me up, but school isn't over yet!

I have a big surprise for you.

At home she tells me and Bibi the news.

Dad is coming home. We're going to pick him up at the airport.

We're so happy as we drive to the airport.

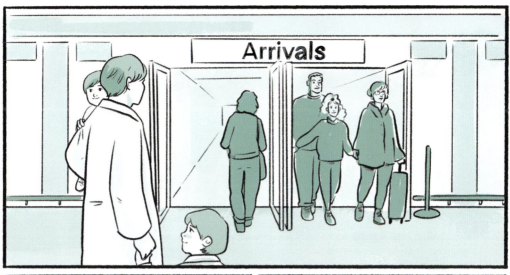

Arrivals

There are lots of people coming out. Where is Dad?

There he is! Daddy!

We are all safe now.

WELCOME

THE
OF W

SOM

WRITTEN BY RAMSEY HASSAN
ILLUSTRATED BY ADA JUSIC

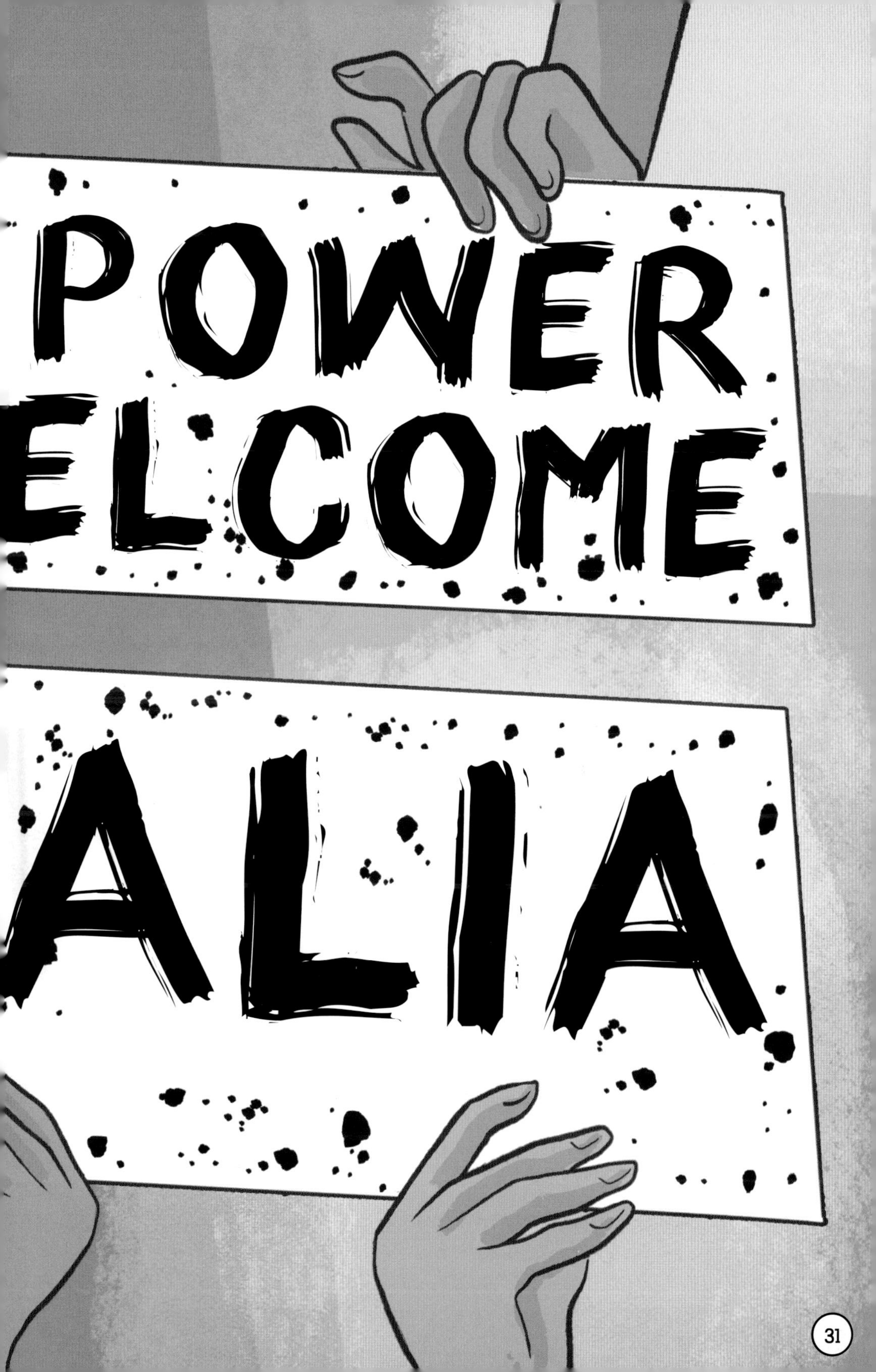
POWER
ELCOME
ALIA

SOMALIA is an East African country. The area is known as the Horn of Africa. Somalia's nearest neighbours are Kenya and Ethiopia, and it has a coastline along the Indian Ocean. It is the longest coastline in mainland Africa. Its capital is Mogadishu, and the majority of Somalis are Muslims. Somalian history dates back to the earliest known human tribes when first humans evolved in Africa up to 2 million years ago. Cave paintings in the northern region of Dhambalin date back 1000–3000 BCE. The Laas Geel cave complex of Hargeisa is roughly five thousand years old.

Other archaeological evidence suggests that Somalia was the site of a civilization that traded with ancient Egypt and Greece. This was probably the fabled Land of Punt, a legendary civilization first mentioned in ancient

Egyptian writings. The region has been a central point for trade for a very long time. Somalia was home to tribes who traded with the Persians, Arabs and the Roman Empire too. They sailed ships called *beden*. They are also thought to have been the first peoples to domesticate camels.

Early Muslims, fleeing persecution in Arabia, introduced Islam to Somalia from around the seventh century CE. The Arab settlers continued to arrive during the Middle Ages, and many married into local clans. By the thirteenth century, the region was ruled by the Ajuran Sultanate. This continued for four centuries, until Ajuran rule ended. The region was divided into smaller sultanates, who continued to trade. They also fought each other for control of the trade routes.

In the nineteenth century, the European powers began to claim colonies across Africa. This was known as the "Scramble for Africa". In 1884, the British created a protectorate in Somalia, on the coast. This was called British Somaliland. Rebels, known as Dervishes, fought

British rule until 1920, when they were eventually defeated. However, Britain was not the only colonial ruler in the region.

Italy created a protectorate in 1889, in the northeast of Somalia. Soon, Italy added the south to their protectorate too. This was called Italian Somaliland. By 1936, Italy's combined colonies became Italian East Africa, and included Ethiopia and Eritrea. All across Africa, countries were invaded and colonized by European powers. However, World War Two was coming, and soon everything would change again. In 1940, with Italy part of Nazi Germany's Axis Powers, the Italians took control of British Somaliland too.

The British retook the colony in 1941 but fought Italian rebel forces until 1943. When the war ended in 1945, much of Somalia remained under British rule. In 1950, the United Nations allowed Italy to regain control of Italian Somaliland, but under UN supervision and with a promise to allow Somalia independence by 1960. This happened on 1 July 1960, with Italian and British colonies uniting under Somali rule. The Somali Republic was created, and ruled by successive presidents.

In 1969, President Abdirashid Ali Shermarke was assassinated. The Somali Army took over the country, led by Mohamed Siad Barre. Barre began to modernize Somalia, and re-established trade links with the Arab world, joining the Arab League in 1974. Before he joined the Arab league, he also strengthened ties with other socialist countries such as the Soviet Union and China. The following year, a severe drought caused mass starvation in Somalia. Barre decided to invade the Ogaden region of Ethiopia in 1977, starting a brutal war. Ethiopia managed to expel Somali troops with help from the Soviet Union and Cuba. In 1977, Barre cut ties with the Soviet Union, and became an ally of the United States. By this time, Barre had become a dictator, and Somalis were not allowed to oppose him.

However, opposition to Barre grew throughout the 1980s. Finally, in 1991, Barre was overthrown. A power struggle began as different groups in Somalia fought for power. Somalia's people suffered greatly and many were killed. In the same year, the former British protectorate, now known as Somaliland, declared independence from Somalia. Although Somaliland, isn't internationally recognized as a country, it has it's own flag and its own political system, government, police force and even its own currency. The founding of Somaliland added to already rising tensions. In 1992, the US troops landed near Mogadishu, Somalia's capital city, as part of a United Nations peacekeeping effort. The goal was to restore order, but the situation grew worse. The US left in March 1994 and in 1995, the United Nations left too, having failed to restore peace. The fighting continued, and many more Somalis were left destitute or lost their lives.

In 2000, Somalia formed its first government since 1991. However, various groups in Somalia refused to accept the new government. Many turned to rebellion. Islamic militants also began to emerge, with the goal of creating an Islamic state in the region. One of the militant groups al-Shabaab had links to al-Qaeda, a group known for terrorist actions. In 2006, Ethiopian troops entered Somalia and helped Somalis to fight back against the militants. Al-Shabaab were pushed back, but they remain a threat.

Despite various new governments since 2000, Somalia is still faced with civil war, and the country has an ongoing humanitarian crisis. Since January 2021, more than one million Somalis have been forced to leave their homes because of drought and famine. Many experts also believe more drought is likely. Over the last few decades, thousands of Somalis have been forced to flee their country. Many of them have faced severe hardship and trauma. Somalis now live in many other countries, including the UK.

Now, everyone! Today's Story Time is going to be very different.

Instead of all of us reading a story together, we're going to be listening to one instead. Three stories, in fact.

Pooja, Hamish and Ramzee are going to tell us stories they've written about refugees.

I want everyone to listen carefully, and if you want to ask a question, please do so after they've finished speaking, OK?

YES, MISS JACOBS.

The stage is yours, Pooja.

Once upon a time there was a frog called Ribbit who lived in a beautiful forest in a faraway country.

But one day the bulldozers came and started destroying the forest. Ribbit lost his friends and family in the confusion. He decided to swim upstream to look for them.

Hungry and alone, Ribbit found a safe place to sleep.

Forty winks and 5,800 miles later...

MUMMY! I don't think this salad you bought is vegan!

What's your name?

Ribbit Puddlegulp.

Uh, how about we call you "Minty" instead?

THE DAILY NEWS
AFRICAN FROG FOUND IN BAG OF MINT!

An RSPCA inspector offered to keep Minty in her home, but the family that found him already loved him, and so Minty now had a home.

What would you do if your home wasn't safe anymore?

It was a normal, boring day. I was playing video games after homework when the bomb fell!

BOOOOOOMM

Home was now a dangerous place, so my parents decided that we should leave and find a new home in a safe country called Haven.

As soon as it got dark, we fled to the docks, where Dad paid a man to let us onto a boat.

My sister didn't survive the journey.

When we arrived, we had to wait to see if we'd be allowed to stay.

We are now safe and happy and I will never call normal "boring" ever again.

I love draw! My father was artist and I loved to watch him paint pictures so much.

He bought me comic book for birthday and I was hooked!

The action! The colours! The art! It so much better than my dull town.

One day, Father went out and did not come back. Mother say he join lot of people to tell president that they want to begin a new country.

But the president no listen and instead put lot of people in jail, including Father.

Feeling unheard, people become rebel and fight president and war begin.

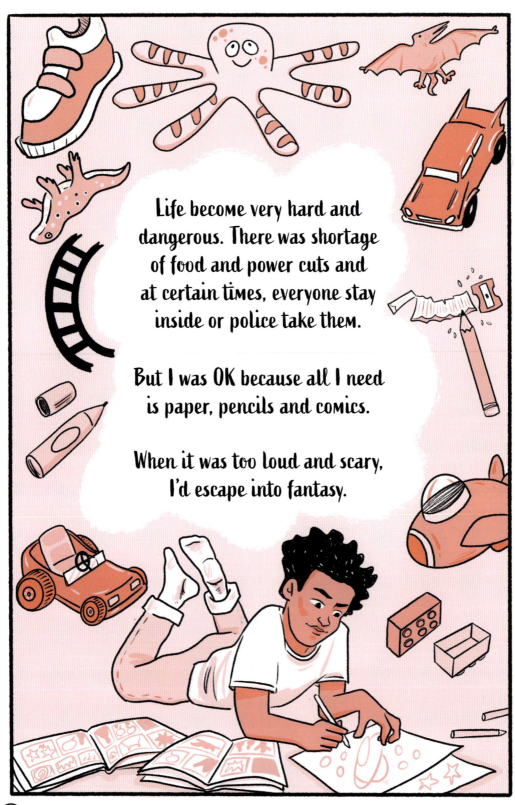

Life become very hard and dangerous. There was shortage of food and power cuts and at certain times, everyone stay inside or police take them.

But I was OK because all I need is paper, pencils and comics.

When it was too loud and scary, I'd escape into fantasy.

Mother managed to get us plane tickets to go somewhere safe.

It was first time on a plane! It was like bus except my ears would go pop and the looking-out window made me feel sick.

But closest open airport was in next region.

When we got off plane, two men take us to room and we were there all day.

Woman ask Mother many questions and make her write on paper a lot.

We put on plane and leave same night.

I sleep bad but I did see a giant clock.

After Mother again asked many questions in room, we leave airport and move to hotel.

Welcome Hotel

Our first home since we leave Somalia.

I learn lot of people who live there also escape dangerous countries.

I crossed a treacherous mountain to escape.

Oh yeah? I was squeezed in the back of a lorry with thirty people and some gross rats for ten hours!

Home 1
Home 2
Home 3
Home 4

Eight months later, council find us home and then another home, and another home. We always moving because no permanent homes available.

I was never at a place long enough to know it or make any firm friends.

Enfield is my fourth home and I be there the longest.

We live in small house on really fun street.

But there's old man who is not nice.

Oh, close the windows, Edna. The Muslims are cooking again!

I love school because it's fun learning new things and my teacher is nice.

My friends here are awesome.

I was invited to my first birthday party.

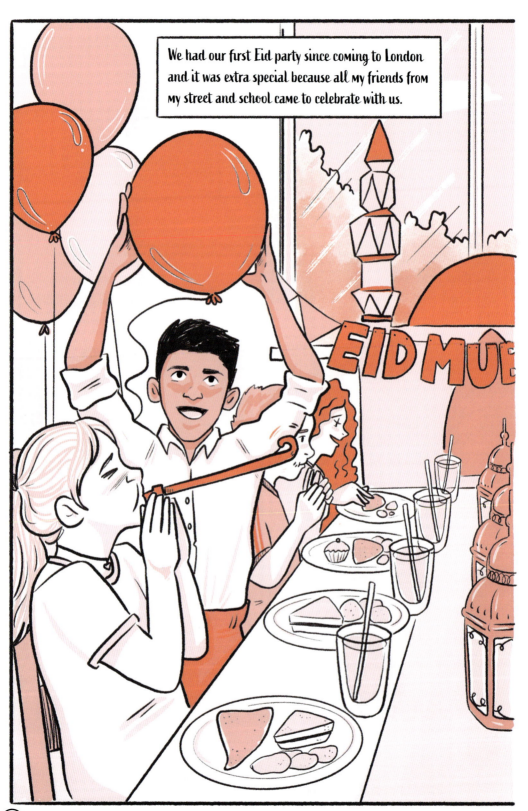

We had our first Eid party since coming to London and it was extra special because all my friends from my street and school came to celebrate with us.

Thanks for listening and asking such wonderful questions. What did you think of the stories?

The frog story was cute.

Ramzee's story. It's interesting because it's real.

The story about the English refugees was scary.

RRRIINNG!!!

YAAAAAY!

We are in the playground. Ramzee is playing pat-ball with a bunch of kids. Pat-ball is like Squash but instead of a racquet, players hit the tennis ball against the wall with their hand.

THE OF W

AFGHA

WRITTEN BY MARIE BAMYANI
ILLUSTRATED BY ADA JUSIC

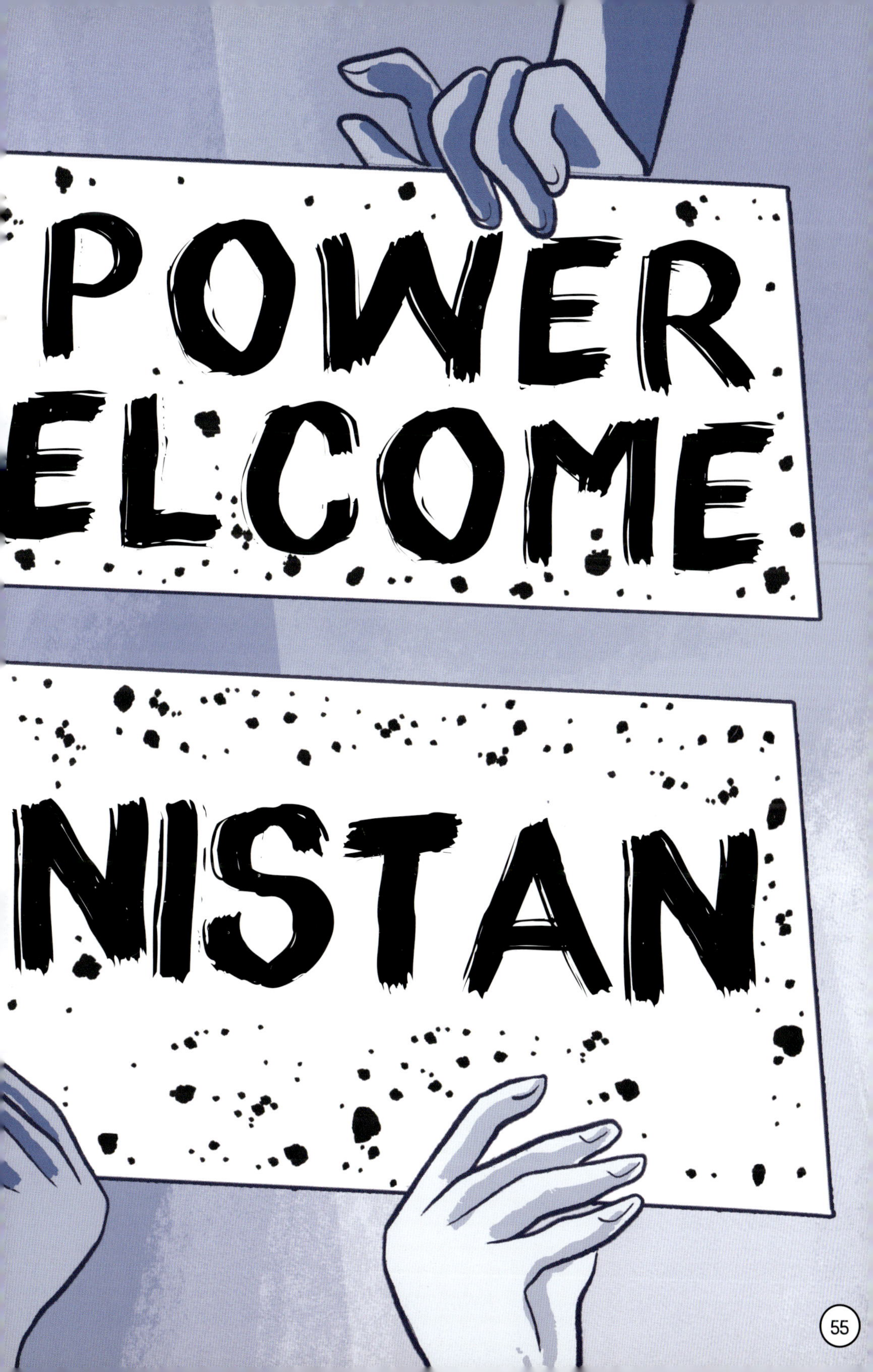

POWER
ELCOME
NISTAN

AFGHANISTAN, a country of rich and varied cultures, is in central South Asia. It is entirely land-locked, and surrounded by the Hindu Kush mountains. It also has many deserts. Its neighbours include Iran and Pakistan. An important trade route between East and West, the country and region has a long history of war. Modern-day Afghanistan is still recovering from the most recent war.

Modern-day Afghanistan didn't exist until 1919. Before that, the land was ruled by many different empires. One of the first to conquer the area was Darius of Babylon, around 500 BCE and many more conquerors followed. In the eleventh century, Mahmūd of Ghazna forged an empire from Iran to India. Each group of invaders left their

mark on the region through language, customs and food. Islam was introduced to the region in the seventh century and is the main religion today. In the twentieth century, there were three British-Afghan Wars, the last of which was in 1919, as the British tried to gain control of the region. The British lost, and an independent Afghanistan was created and led by Amīr Amānullāh Khan.

However, in 1926, Khan turned Afghanistan into a monarchy and declared himself king. Khan wanted to reform girls' education. He tried to win support for his reforms from the Loya Jirga (a national tribal council) in 1928 but his plan backfired and civil war broke out. In 1929, Khan abdicated, and in 1933 after a period of unrest and instability a new king, Zahir Shah, was appointed.

Zahir ruled for forty years and tried to modernize and stabilize Afghanistan. At first, Zahir tried to pay for new developments out of the country's own wealth, but he soon realised that they needed aid (money from another country) to make the changes he wanted, and so Zahir and his prime minister, Daud Khan, turned to the Soviet Union for aid and military assistance.

The Soviet leader, Nikita Khrushchev, sent aid to Afghanistan in 1956, as the two countries became allies. Zahir reformed women's rights, so that they could work and attend university. Many Afghans welcomed modernization, but some were fiercely critical of reforms, especially greater rights for women. Opposition to Daud and King Zahir, began to grow. In 1965, a communist party was formed in secret.

In 1973, Daud Khan overthrew Zahir to become president of Afghanistan and abolished the monarchy. Although Daud further reformed women's rights, he also started to attack his opponents. Those who opposed him were sacked from the government and many were silenced. In 1978, a coup resulted in his death and the Afghan Communist Party took control.

The new president, Nur Mohammed Taraki, distanced Afghanistan from the Soviet Union. Other members of the Communist Party objected to Taraki's plans and opposed him. Meanwhile, in the countryside, religious leaders and clans who objected to reforms began an armed struggle. They became known as the Mujahideen. In 1979, the country began to fall apart.

First, the US ambassador to Afghanistan was killed. In September 1979, President Taraki was killed. Chaos erupted. On 24 December, the Soviet Union invaded Afghanistan, and in the countryside, the Mujahideen groups joined forces to fight the invasion. The war would last for a decade.

There were two sides: the Afghan Communist Party and the Mujahideen. The Afghan Communist Party was supported by the Soviet Union and their allies while the Mujahideen were supported and funded by the US, the UK and China. One of the Mujahideen commanders was the notorious Osama bin Laden. The Soviets struggled to gain ground in the countryside. As a result, they could not control Afghanistan and, in 1988, a peace treaty was signed and the Soviets withdrew. The Mujahideen took over various parts of the country, but they too began to fight among themselves.

Soon, the US and UK stopped funding the Mujahideen, which angered many fighters, including Osama bin Laden. After a series of battles with other clans, the Taliban took control of Afghanistan. They were a religious movement who believed that Afghanistan should be ruled under Islamic Sharia laws. Women were forbidden from work and education. They also had to cover their faces in public.

The Taliban let Osama bin Laden and his terrorist group, called al-Qaeda, hide in Afghanistan after they launched a series of attacks across the US on 11 September 2001. Many of the attacks targeted government buildngs, such as the Pentagon but the US's World Trade Centre was also attacked and destroyed. The US launched an attack on Afghanistan, leading to a disastrous war. Civilians lost their homes and many fled the country. Eventually the Taliban government was overthrown.

The violence didn't end. Thousands of US troops remained in Afghanistan, and the Taliban and al-Qaeda joined forces to attack them and President Hamid Karzai's newly elected government. In 2014, the US ended its operations, but US military personnel remained. The Taliban continued to undermine the Afghan government, often through violence.

In 2021, the last of the US troops left. However, the Taliban were waiting. The Afghan government had already collapsed and the Taliban regained control of the country. Refugees from Afghanistan have fled across the world throughout the past forty years, with many settling in the UK. The future of Afghanistan is uncertain, and its history suggests that the chances for peace are slim.

As I pour myself a cup of tea, the sunlight entering my room reminds me of late afternoons in Kabul. But there is no comparison between the taste of the tea here in Germany and the taste of tea back home.

Here, even the taste of tea is a reminder of displacement.

MUHAJIR

I first learned the word muhajir – immigrant – when I was I six years old. Back then, I didn't know exactly what it meant, but I had always wondered why our school was different from other schools.

Why does my school only have one room?

Why doesn't my school have a playground?

Why are the textbooks so boring?

Because we are immigrants. It feels like we're not considered humans in this country and have no rights.

Now, twenty years on, I have returned to the same starting point.

The only difference is that I am no longer a child and can feel with all my soul what it means to be a refugee, an immigrant, a displaced person.

I try to enjoy the beautiful surroundings here. But every time I look at the sky, I remember the people who rushed to the airport to escape when Kabul fell.

Or when I look at the traffic, my heart beats faster, the memories of bombs in Kabul flooding back.

15 AUGUST 2021

I woke up thinking it was a normal day that day. But on my way to the office, I noticed there was more traffic than usual.

I looked at the faces of the people. They were tired and terrified and fleeing in despair.

I didn't know why, but I decided I should head home.

What's wrong with everyone? Where are they going?

The Taliban have reached Kabul.

Don't spread rumours.

I stopped breathing and my head started spinning. My vision went black.

But then I looked out of the window and saw that it was true.

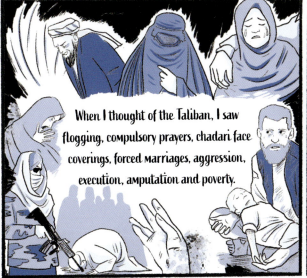

When I thought of the Taliban, I saw flogging, compulsory prayers, chadari face coverings, forced marriages, aggression, execution, amputation and poverty.

BANG! BANG! BANG!

That night, I waited for a knock at our door. I thought we would be the Taliban's next targets.

On social media, I saw a clip of a man falling from a plane.

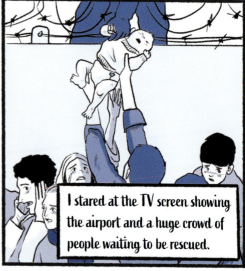

I stared at the TV screen showing the airport and a huge crowd of people waiting to be rescued.

The sound of shooting dispersed everyone for a few minutes and then there was blood, wounded people and crying.

But the people gathered again, as if death no longer scared them.

I called my friend.

The people fleeing the airport trampled on me. They've injured my legs.

I didn't dare go to the airport.

Some people took selfies with the Taliban. I wondered if it was because they were having a hard time believing the reality of the situation.

Justice and freedom!

We are not the women of twenty years ago.

Women started to protest against the Taliban.

One of my friends added me to a women's WhatsApp group to plan future protests. The group was full of photos of women being beaten up while protesting.

There were also warnings.

I burned my books and documents and my workplace ID card so they didn't fall into the hands of the Taliban.

I didn't know how long it had been since the Taliban came to power, but I needed to go to the city to withdraw money.

Stand and wait in the corner with the others.

The Taliban attacked a girl, but her family can't speak up because it will bring shame on them.

The Taliban took away a neighbour's son last night. Nobody knows where he is.

I don't know what we've done to deserve this. We've gone to sleep hungry for several nights because my husband is a labourer and can't find work now.

The women were whispering to one another.

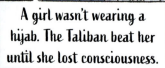

A girl wasn't wearing a hijab. The Taliban beat her until she lost consciousness.

The people in the city were all wandering around like lost souls. Nobody was thinking about the future. The people had dug a grave for themselves and were waiting for their turn to be buried.

I went to the Ministry of Higher Education with my friend.

We've come for our educational documents.

What documents?! You can't work or study any more.

We have no intention of working with this group.

Can we have our documents or not?

When the guard reached for his gun, I got scared and told my friend we should leave.

We went back the following week and the week after and the week after that. The same story repeated. Finally, a friend helped us to get our documents.

If there is an uprising here, I'll fight with my heart and soul.

It raised a glimmer of hope in my heart to hear about the uprisings against the Taliban in some districts.

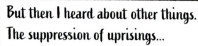

But then I heard about other things. The suppression of uprisings...

the destruction of statues and graves...

the closure of Shia mosques...

the forcible imposing of taxes...

killings, kidnappings, torture...
... and my heart became heavy again.

What kind of future could I have under this regime, which sees women as pieces of meat?

In the end, I decided I had to leave. The truth is that it is extremely difficult to live under the same sky as the Taliban.

I left my family, Kabul and my whole life behind with a suitcase weighing twenty kilograms.

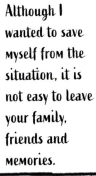

Although I wanted to save myself from the situation, it is not easy to leave your family, friends and memories.

I might be filled with fury, hatred and sadness for a long time. I am always accompanied by the sad eyes of my family.

I arrived in Germany on 6 November. It was my birthday. I congratulated myself on beginning a new life of loneliness.

I live in a one-bedroom flat in a small but beautiful city. The people here are so kind.

When my bicycle broke down, my language teacher took me to a bike mechanic.

This one's for free.

Are you sure? I can afford to pay.

You're new to the city – please – it's on the house.

Every time we bump into each other on the street, he asks about my bicycle.

My shop is always open to you!

Another time, a doctor invited me to her house for tea.

And a caring, older man made me coffee at his workshop. The workshop smelled of fuel and burnt cooking oil.

It is with these simple gestures of love, not mercy or pity, that humans give one another hope.

These days, our city is filled with sympathy for Ukraine.

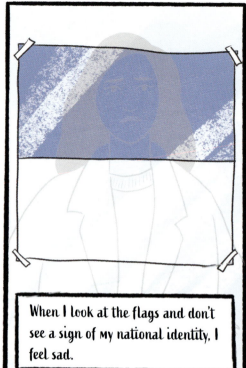

When I look at the flags and don't see a sign of my national identity, I feel sad.

Sometimes, I think that an immigrant or a refugee from an Eastern country belongs nowhere, not even to their birthplace.

They are always displaced and drifting, just like a piece of wood in the middle of the sea. Would my situation be like this if I hadn't been born in Afghanistan?

When I signed at the bottom of the form to receive my residence card, the officer was surprised that I could read English. But this is nothing new.

Often when I speak English, and talk about my studies and work, the very first question that I get asked is where I am from.

I'm from Afghanistan.

I have been friends with many refugees from Afghanistan, but none were so highly educated.

When I answer, I see surprised faces.

My residence card is valid for three years. I am very happy that I am legally allowed to study and work.

I have started to make plans and dream of a good future. I am truly happy that I can live in Germany as an immigrant, benefit from all its laws and enjoy its privileges, things that I barely benefited from in my own land because of my ethnicity as a Hazara.

The variety of cultures and ethnicities in this country are so fascinating that I sometimes wish there were no borders. Maybe then we humans would never feel like strangers to one another.

THE
OF W

UKR

WRITTEN BY SONYA ZHURENKO
ILLUSTRATED BY ADA JUSIC

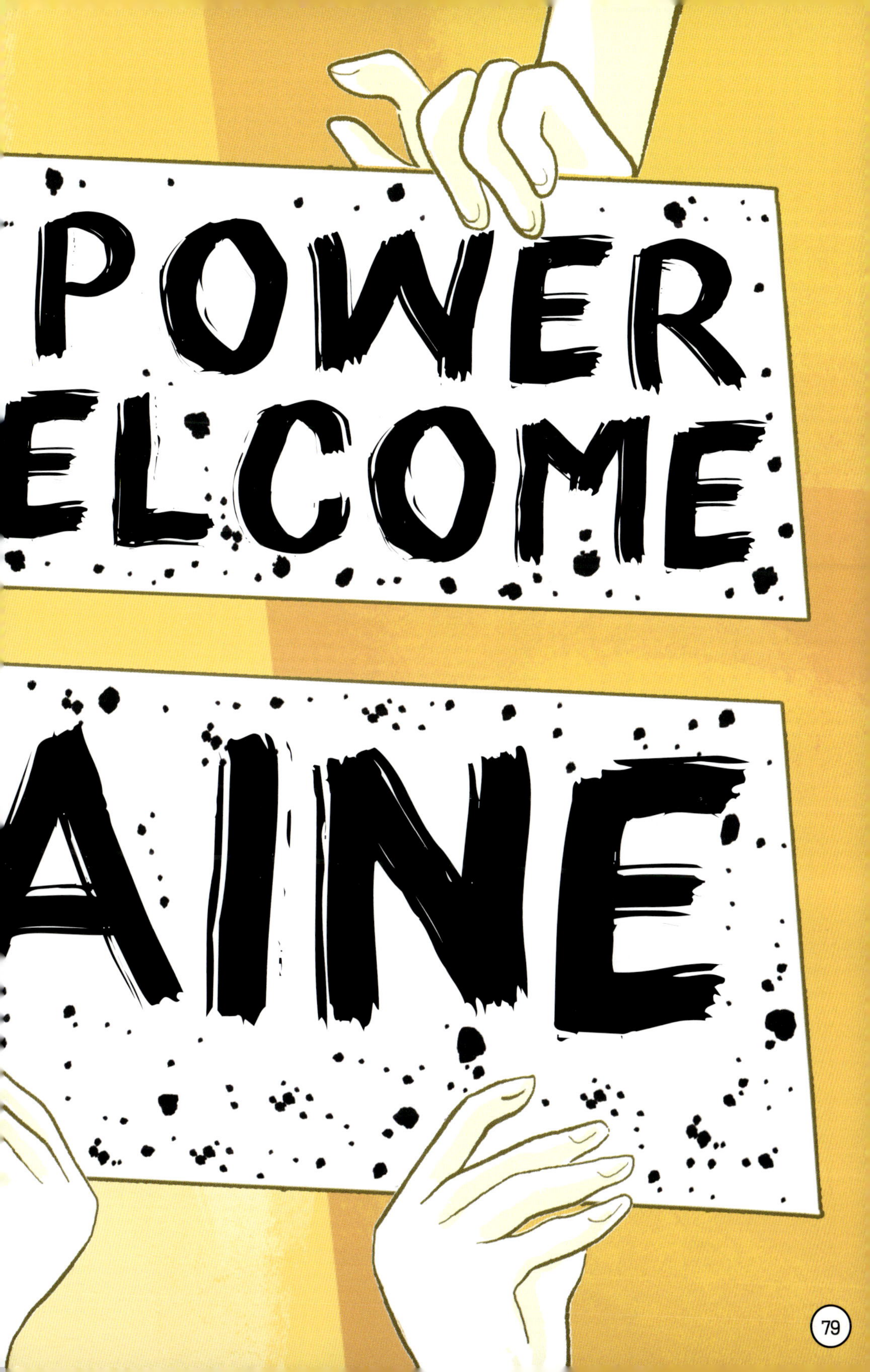
POWER
ELCOME
AINE

UKRAINE is a country in eastern Europe with a varied history. Its neighbours include Russia, which has often ruled the country in recent times. Russia invaded Ukraine in February 2022. Throughout its history, Ukraine has been conquered and invaded many times. Ukraine's capital is Kyiv (or Kiev), a city of great beauty and rich culture. Ukraine has huge natural resources such as coal, gas, iron, timber, sunflower seeds and much more.

In the seventh century BCE, people known as the Cimmerians, Scythians and Sarmatians lived in what is now Ukraine. At this time, the Greeks also created colonies along the Black Sea coastline of what is now modern-day Ukraine. Around the same time, this area was occupied by the Cimmerians, followed by the Scythians and then the Sarmatians, who all originated from Iran. Around the sixth century CE, the Slavs arrived and settled. No one is sure where the Slavs originated, but Slavic people can be found throughout eastern Europe including in what is now Russia, Czech Republic, Slovakia, Poland, Croatia, Serbia and Ukraine. Around the ninth century CE, Varangians (Vikings) from Scandinavia (Denmark, Norway and Sweden) helped to found a new state called Kyivan Rus. Their leader, Oleg, ruled Novgorod (in what is now Russia) and decided to take control of Kyiv too. Oleg became knowns as Prince Oleg of Kyiv. The Vikings were keen merchants, warriors and traders, and made Kyiv the capital of their new state. In 988, Vladimir the Great converted the region to Christianity.

After this, Kyivan Rus's power declined for a couple of centuries. By the twelfth century CE, the region was broken into smaller states. In the thirteenth century CE, Mongols and Tatars from Asia began to invade. In 1240, the Golden Horde, a part of the Mongol Empire, attacked Kyiv and looted the city. They conquered the south and east of the country. In the fourteenth century, Lithuania and Poland began to expand into Ukraine. The Mongols remained in east Crimea, which became the Khanate of Crimea and then became part of the Ottoman Empire. The Ottomans were Muslims and there remains a minority Muslim population in Ukraine to this day.

In the fifteenth and sixteenth centuries, areas of Ukraine were settled by the Cossacks. Some believe the Cossacks were runaway serfs or slaves, and others think they were people who left existing settlements to find new land, usually the wild steppe (grassland) region, where they could make their own rules. The Cossacks were fierce warriors, and although most were Orthodox Christians, anyone could join them. The

Cossacks formed self-governing communities and later the Cossack Hetmanate – a mini-state.

However, by the eighteenth century, Russia controlled eastern Ukraine, and the Cossack Hetmanate was abolished. With Poland's power in western Ukraine failing, Russia took control, annexing Crimea in 1783. Most of Ukraine was now under Russian control. Into the nineteenth century, Ukrainian nationalists began to call for independence from Russia. For a brief time, from 1918, Ukraine did gain independence, but in 1921, Russia (now part of the Soviet Union) regained control. The Soviet leader, Joseph Stalin, introduced rapid industrialization and forced

Ukraine to grow more grain to supply the Soviet Union. But the Ukrainian farmers could not keep up, and the Soviets confiscated grain, leaving Ukraine in a terrible famine. Millions of ordinary Ukrainians suffered and died in what is known as the Holodomor (meaning the Great Famine).

In 1941, Nazi Germany invaded Ukraine and the atrocities continued. When the Soviets regained Kyiv in 1943, that suffering did not end. Instead, Stalin sent anyone who opposed his rule to labour camps or prisons. After the war, Ukraine remained part of the Soviet Union. In 1986, a terrible accident at the Chernobyl nuclear power station devastated the surrounding area. Radiation contaminated nearly 150,000 square kilometres, and the area immediately around Chernobyl was made uninhabitable.

In 1991, the Soviet Union collapsed. A referendum in December 1991 saw ninety-three per cent of Ukrainians back independence. Now free from Soviet rule, Ukraine had its first presidential election. However, Ukraine's economy suffered in the early 1990s, and many people were forced into poverty. Corruption scandals in government made people angry and suspicious.

After the 2004 presidential election, people turned against the winner, Viktor Yanukovych, who was close to Russia's leaders. The opposition claimed that the election was rigged in Yanukovych's favour and took their protests to the streets. Eventually, the election results were overturned. A new election saw the opposition leader, Viktor Yushchenko, declared president. This became known as the Orange Revolution. Russia's leaders were unhappy with the result, and tensions between Ukraine and Russia increased.

In February and March 2014, Russia illegally annexed Crimea and claimed the territory as its own. This led to a huge rise in tensions, and Russia was condemned across the worlds for its actions. However, the Russians claimed that Crimea was a majority Russian-speaking region, and always part of Russia itself. The problems continued and in February 2022, Russia invaded Ukraine. Despite again being condemned by most other countries, the Russians continued to attack Ukrainian targets in Kyiv and elsewhere. This led to a refugee crisis, with many Ukrainians being left homeless. Some of those refugees have been welcomed into other European countries, including the UK.

The night before everything began, I couldn't fall asleep for a long time.

Picnic?

Sounds good!

My friends and I had planned a picnic in the park. But in the end, we never got to go.

We should go swimming!

And go shopping!

All winter, we'd looked forward to the summer. We had a long list of things we wanted to do.

Unfortunately, now we won't see each other for a very long time.

At first, I didn't hear anything. It was so quiet that you might have thought the announcement that active operations had begun was a joke.

Then explosions were heard in the distance.

RUSSIA-UKRAINE CRISIS
RESIDENTIAL AREA IN KEY CITY
HIT BY RUSSIAN AIRSTRIKES

Watching the news was like torture.

My family spent a long time thinking about whether it was worth it to go away.

Where would we go?

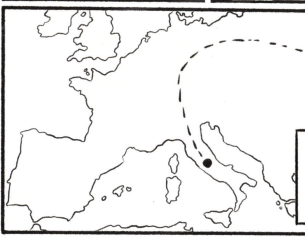

After lots of long discussions, my grandad and my mum came to the agreement that Italy was the best option for us.

We packed up our things and left our home.

At the train station, we joined the long queue to catch a train.

We were sent to a compartment where there were already nine people.

We took it in turns to sleep.

I was lucky that there were only two people on the top shelf. I climbed up and got as comfortable as I could.

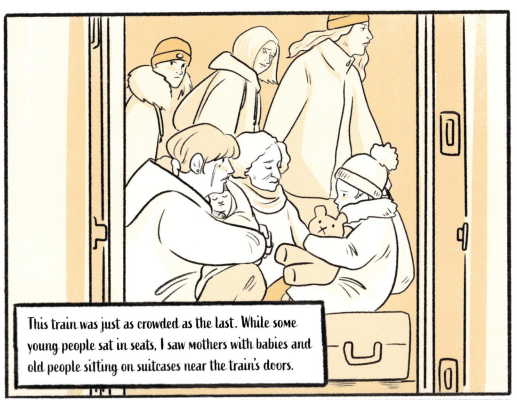

This train was just as crowded as the last. While some young people sat in seats, I saw mothers with babies and old people sitting on suitcases near the train's doors.

It was cold. People tried to wrap up their children in all kinds of rugs and blankets, but this didn't seem to help much.

We got off the train late at night.

We were registered and sent on a direct flight to Warsaw, the capital of Poland.

Fortunately, the conditions on the plane were more comfortable than those on the trains.

In Warsaw, a bus picked us up and took us to a huge building, which had been converted into a place to sleep.

There were thousands of camp beds and just as many people.

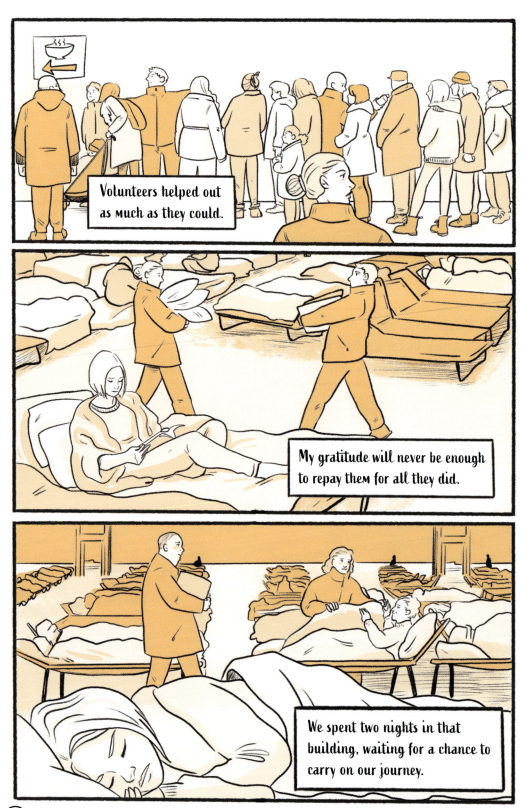

Volunteers helped out as much as they could.

My gratitude will never be enough to repay them for all they did.

We spent two nights in that building, waiting for a chance to carry on our journey.

Eventually, we caught a bus that was heading to Italy.

Outside the window, the landscapes changed from windmills to multi-storey buildings.

Vítejte v Praze!

WILLKOMMEN IN WIEN

We spent the night in the Czech Republic and Austria before finally crossing the border into Italy.

Once in the city, in the midst of magnificent mountains, our group was settled in a hotel for refugees.

For the first few days, I felt very bad. My body wasn't used to all the changes.

I could neither eat nor sleep.

There's a family who are ready to host a mother with two children in their house.

This was our chance.

The road to Milan was long and tiring. We were met at the train station and taken to Como, an Italian city on the edge of a huge lake.

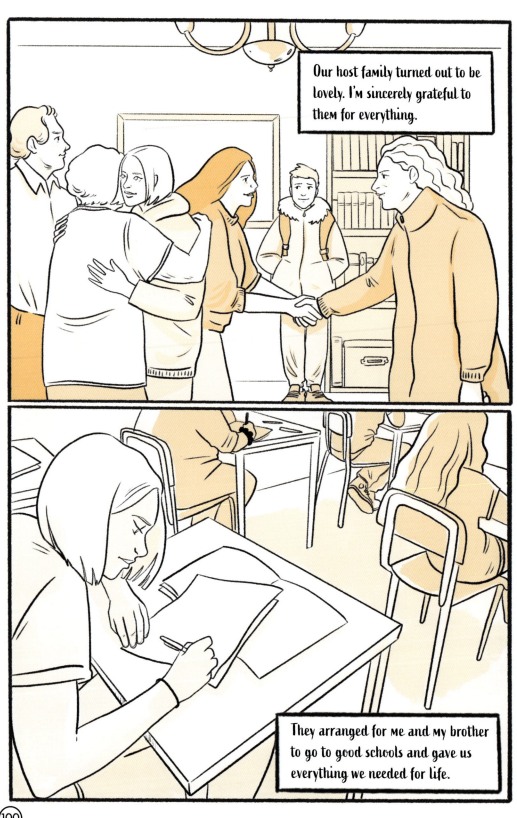

Our host family turned out to be lovely. I'm sincerely grateful to them for everything.

They arranged for me and my brother to go to good schools and gave us everything we needed for life.

THE
OF W
SY

WRITTEN BY NADINE KAADAN
ILLUSTRATED BY ADA JUSIC

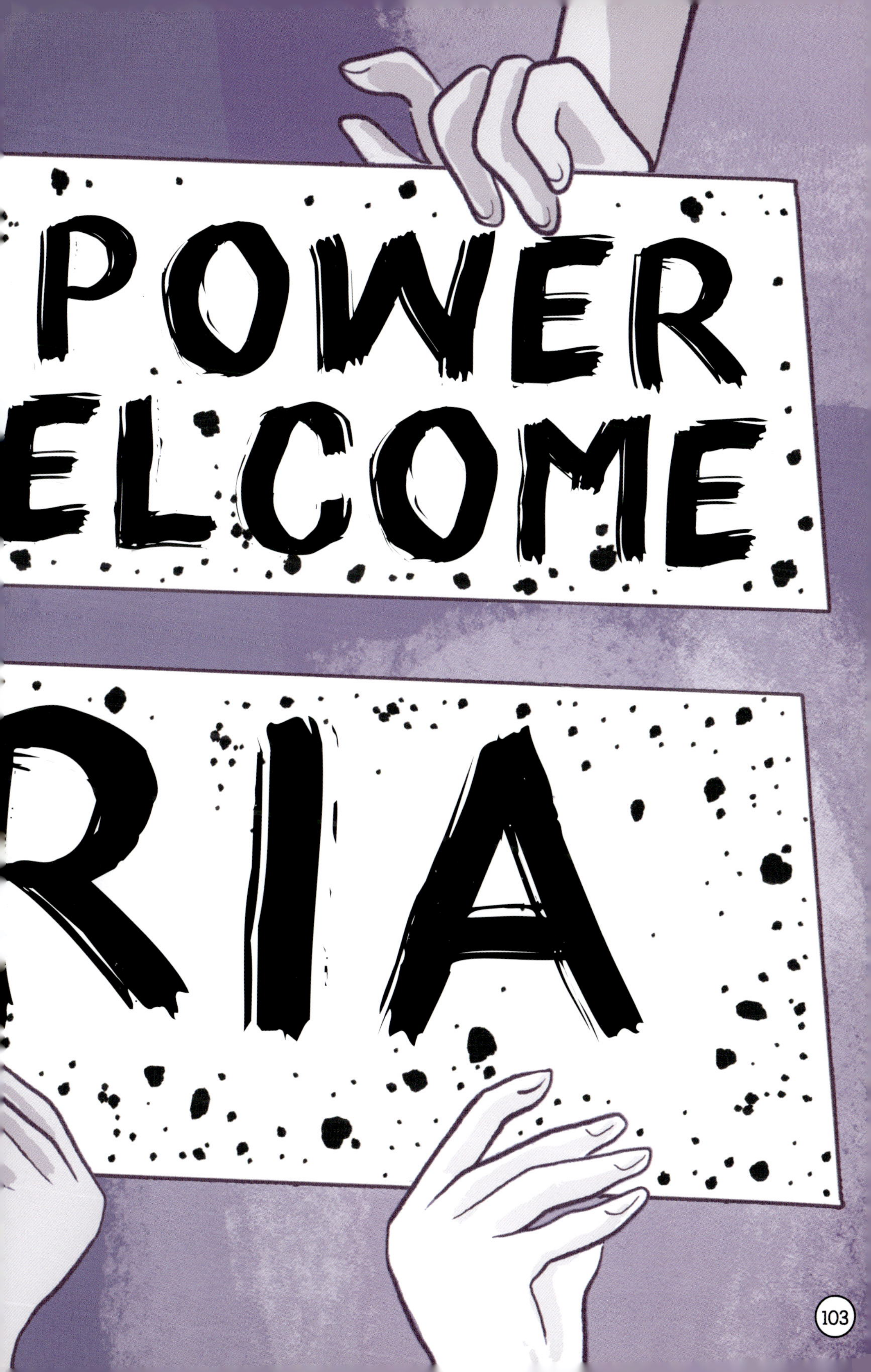
POWER
ELCOME
RIA

Beyond and despite the recent troubles, Syria remains a country of truly unique beauty and immense charm - with those who have visited tending to stay connected to it in some meaningful way for the rest of their lives. Geographically, while it seems that every country likes to think of itself as the place where East meets West, Syria can actually make a convincing case for it. Commonly thought of as the beating heart of the Arab world, Syria sits on the lush eastern Mediterranean Sea with Turkey to its north, and the Arabian Penninsula to its south, and was for centuries one of the westernmost points on the silk and spice roads as goods, peoples and cultures from China and other East Asian countries made their way through what is now modern-day Syria to Venice and then the rest of Europe, and vice-versa.

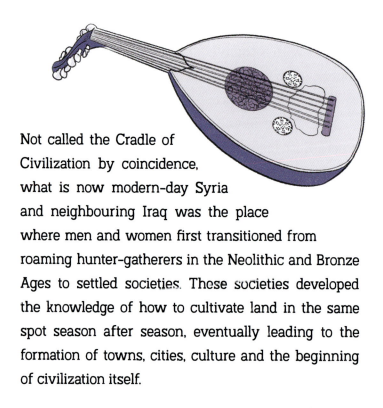

Not called the Cradle of Civilization by coincidence, what is now modern-day Syria and neighbouring Iraq was the place where men and women first transitioned from roaming hunter-gatherers in the Neolithic and Bronze Ages to settled societies. These societies developed the knowledge of how to cultivate land in the same spot season after season, eventually leading to the formation of towns, cities, culture and the beginning of civilization itself.

This was a key evolutionary step in human civilization we take for granted today, and it took place between the Syrian Euphrates and Iraqi Tigris rivers, marking the dawn of humankind's earliest civilization, the Sumerian (around 4,000 BCE) which thrived on the fertile soil along those rivers. In fact, as Syria's capital city, Damascus is the oldest continuously inhabited city in the world and can speak of 9,000 years of history. Its ancient old town is beautiful and transporting in equal measure, making one feel as if they've suddenly travelled back in time a thousand years or two.

Syria's much coveted geography was (and continues) to prove both a blessing and a curse, as it meant that countless civilizations and empires brought with them the fortunes and misfortunes of knowledge, war, culture, wealth, hardship and always change. Competing control of the land came from the Egyptians from the south, the Hittites from the north and the Persians and Babylonians from the east. As for control of the strategic trade routes along the coast, the Canaanites and Phoenicians battled. Each of these empires brought their own cutting edge technologies and inventions to the region. The Phoenicians, for example, were the first in history to develop glass, and in Ugarit, tablets of the first alphabet written in the fourteenth century BCE were found, a first building block in the development of other written languages such as Latin, Greek, Hebrew, Arabic and Aramaic – the language that Jesus spoke. Incredibly Aramaic is still spoken in three villages in Syria – some of the last communities that speak it in the world.

Three Roman emperors originated from within the borders of present-day Syria, and Queen Zenobia of Palmyra (one of the earliest feminist icons in history) was a more than worthy rival to the Roman Empire in the third century CE, though the eastern Roman (or Byzantine) Empire based in Constantinople (now Istanbul) eventually recovered the region. By the seventh century, Damascus became the epicentre of the Umayyad Empire, the beginning of a seven-century period of Islamic dynasties that ushered in a golden age of innovation in sciences, medicine, technology and the arts – at a time when Europe was yet to emerge from the Middle ages – with legacies that still resonate today. An example of this includes the invention of the astrolabe, a beautiful device that signified a revolution in astrology and navigation. Another was the invention of algebra, allowing mathematicians, architects and engineers to solve much more complex problems in their fields. During the fourteenth century came more change with the rise of the Ottoman Empire that would hold power for almost 600 years, until its demise in WW1 at the hands of the British and French Empires that would take its place through the end of WW2, until they were expelled by Syrian revolutionaries after a long and hard-fought struggle for freedom from Imperialism. This ushered in modern-day Syria's period of self-rule from 1946 onwards, one characterized by periods of interchanging turbulence and stability, socialist-leaning politics, support of Palestinian rights and, now, a brutal conflict that places Syria at the mercy of international geo-politics once again.

Beyond its ancient and storied history, and its sparkling culture and arts, Syria's richest and most fascinating asset is undoubtedly its people, who have given much to the civilized world. Witty, playful and warm, they seem always ready with an inviting smile that pulls you in to their homes and their hearts, for the guest is, above all and as per tradition, to be deeply honoured and welcomed. As the descendants of countless civilizations and witnesses to history itself, they pride themselves on their social and religious tolerance, coexisting in friendship and warmth. And they continue to contribute beauty and legacy, from the dulcet tones of singer Asmahan strumming her Oud (the precursor to the guitar), to the poetry of Nizar Kabbani, and powerhouse performances of Sabah Fakhri (who holds the Guinness World Record for singing continuously without pause – 10 hours!). However, the tragic conflict this past decade has meant that over 600,000 Syrians have sadly lost their lives, with over half the population of 23 million displaced either internally or externally. Over sixty per cent of all urban areas are either destroyed or damaged, and an economic crisis has ensured that over ninety per cent of all Syrians now live below the poverty line. 'Resilience' is a word that is often overused today, but Syrians have truly earned it – they have earned this most problematic of compliments. The war has been hard on all Syrians, some much more than others, but time will no doubt ensure that it is temporary, and that Syria will sparkle again. As the author and illustrator Nadine Kaadan often says: "We will never let the conflict colour who we are and what we can be."

Where are you from?

Syria.

Oh my God! Syria? But your English is so good!

And you look very western and modern!

I wanted to scream...

I speak Arabic, French and English just fine and I look Syrian, thank you very much!

...but I didn't.

I let his words to go through me like bullets. Toy bullets, of course.

The kind that hurt and annoy you for a minute or two but then you ignore the sting.

I joked but he didn't laugh.

And how is it you have blue eyes when you're Muslim?

Women aren't forbidden from having blue eyes in Islam as far as I'm aware!

Syria has a beautiful mix of people — and dozens of sects and religions and endless colour.

It quickly became clear to me that a migrant or refugee is fascinating to people.

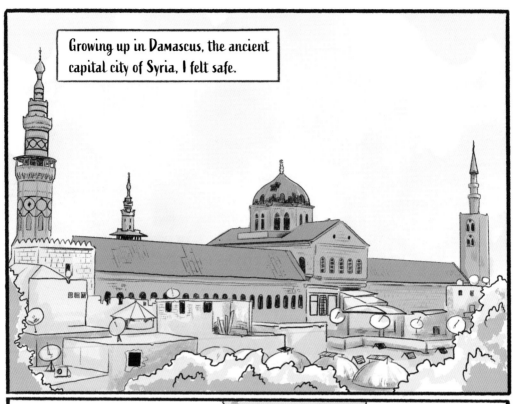

Growing up in Damascus, the ancient capital city of Syria, I felt safe.

It was always peaceful.

We would hang out around the ancient fountains...

...and grab vanilla and pistachio ice cream from Bakdash – the oldest ice cream shop in the world.

We never thought anything would change.

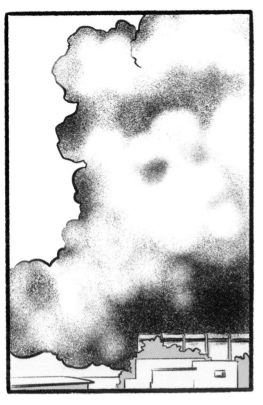

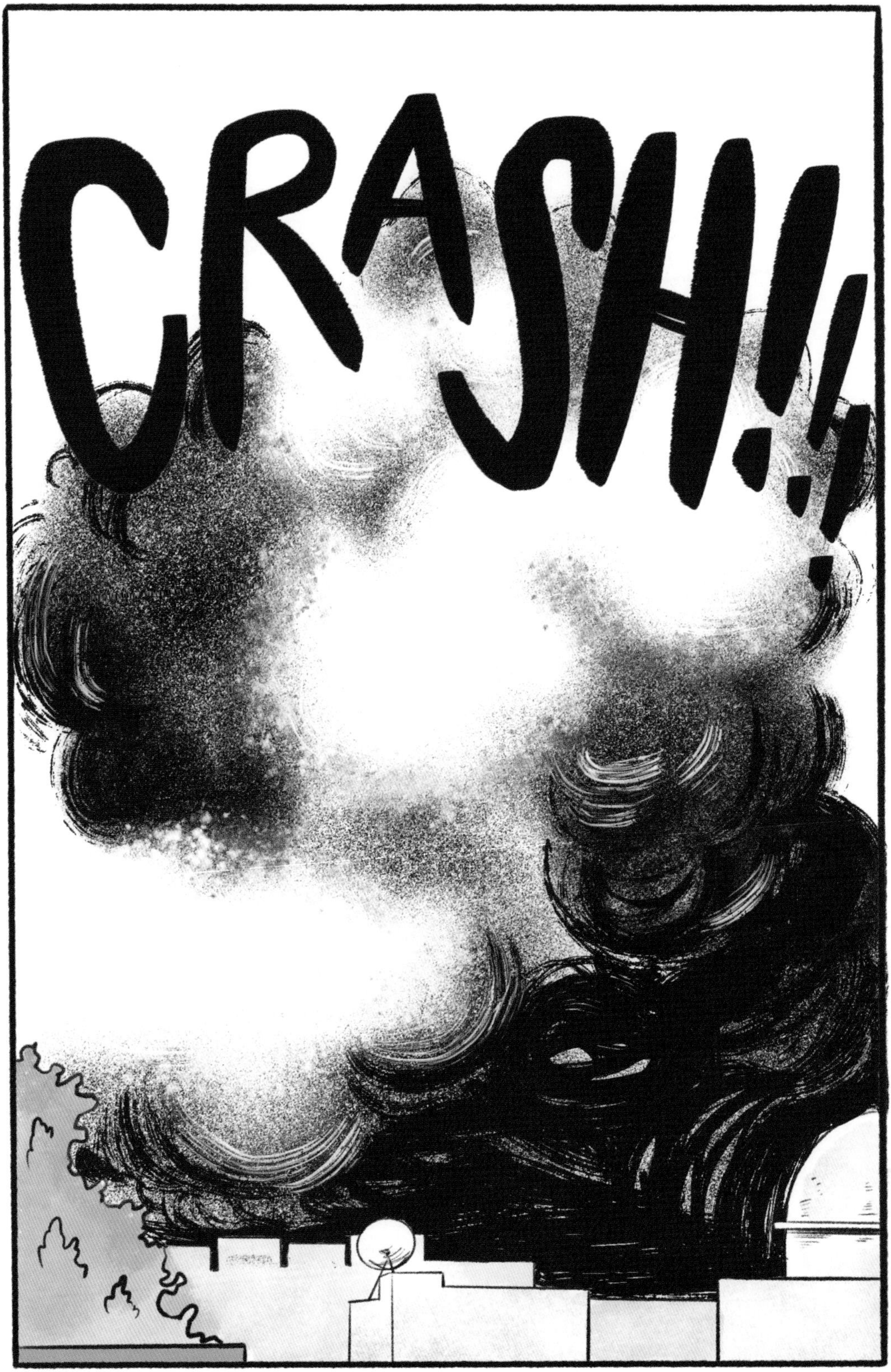
CRASH!!!

Suddenly, there were terrifying explosions every night. We wondered if – and when – they would reach us.

Our streets soon became littered with soldiers...

and checkpoints where cars would be stopped and inspected...

Images of bombed-out buildings on the news became normal.

The fighting in Damascus's suburbs was intense. People were shocked and terrified.

A curfew might be imposed.

The fighting is getting a lot closer to us...

We need to prepare for that and start stocking up on food.

Go to the shops as quickly as you can.

And buy more than you think we need so we can share with neighbours.

What do we need to survive a lockdown during war?

I went with my friend to the supermarket. We both stared at the aisles, not knowing what to buy.

Chocolate ice cream!

We stocked up on ice cream, crisps and mustard for sandwiches, obviously. We thought we were ready for anything.

But when my mum saw what we bought, she wasn't happy.

During wartime we need to buy lots of dry food! It's easy to store and lasts a long time.

Things like lentils, pasta, rice and burgul.

Being stuck at home was hard, but being stuck with such boring food was brutal. We would soon discover that this was the least of our worries...

ENTIRE FAMILY DISAPPEARED...

YOUNG STUDENT DEAD...

YOUNG BOY KIDNAPPED FOR RANSOM MONEY

I dreaded looking at social media but it became my morning ritual because it was where we got our news about the war, as it was faster than the news on TV. Every day, someone we knew was found dead or had disappeared.

Even so, I never expected to see a picture of my friend.

I couldn't breathe for a few seconds.

STUDENT RAMI TRAGICALLY KILLED IN BOMBING...

rest in power Rami

RIP Rami ♥

The black banner on Rami's photo meant he had died.

It was a pain unlike any other. I stopped checking my phone. At least it delayed terrible news for a short while.

Much more fortunate than most, we were able to book a flight to London.

On the flight to London I had so many burning questions. I didn't understand why I was different to the people around me. How could a European passport give me the right to move freely? Why could I choose to leave war behind while my friends couldn't?

I'm blessed to have lived in Syria all my life, but by a strange twist of fate I also happened to be a dual citizen – something that might have saved my life.

As winter deepened though, I got quite tired. I felt that I had needed to explain my existence and my appearance.

STATION COFFEE

It was especially difficult to do so on cold and dark London mornings after an overpriced (and tasteless) coffee from the station.

New Cross 3m
Crystal Palace 10m

I felt that no matter how many strange questions I answered about our lives back home, mostly to show our similarities, being different seemed more reassuring to people here.

The war raged on. We stayed another year.

And another.

And another ... to this day.

It's pouring it down, isn't it?

Today, I queue like a Londoner. I've learnt to like tasteless filter coffee.

I even practise the national pastime of moaning about the weather.

Over time, I stopped feeling like a stranger. Now, this wonderful, hectic city feels like home.

I'm incredibly lucky because I'm still able to visit Syria as often as I can to see my family and friends there.

Travelling back always reminds me of how resilient our people are, how beautiful our country is and how incredibly rich our cultural heritage is – despite everything. No matter how long I stay in London, I will never let this brutal – but temporary – war colour who I am or make me forget the magic of where I come from.

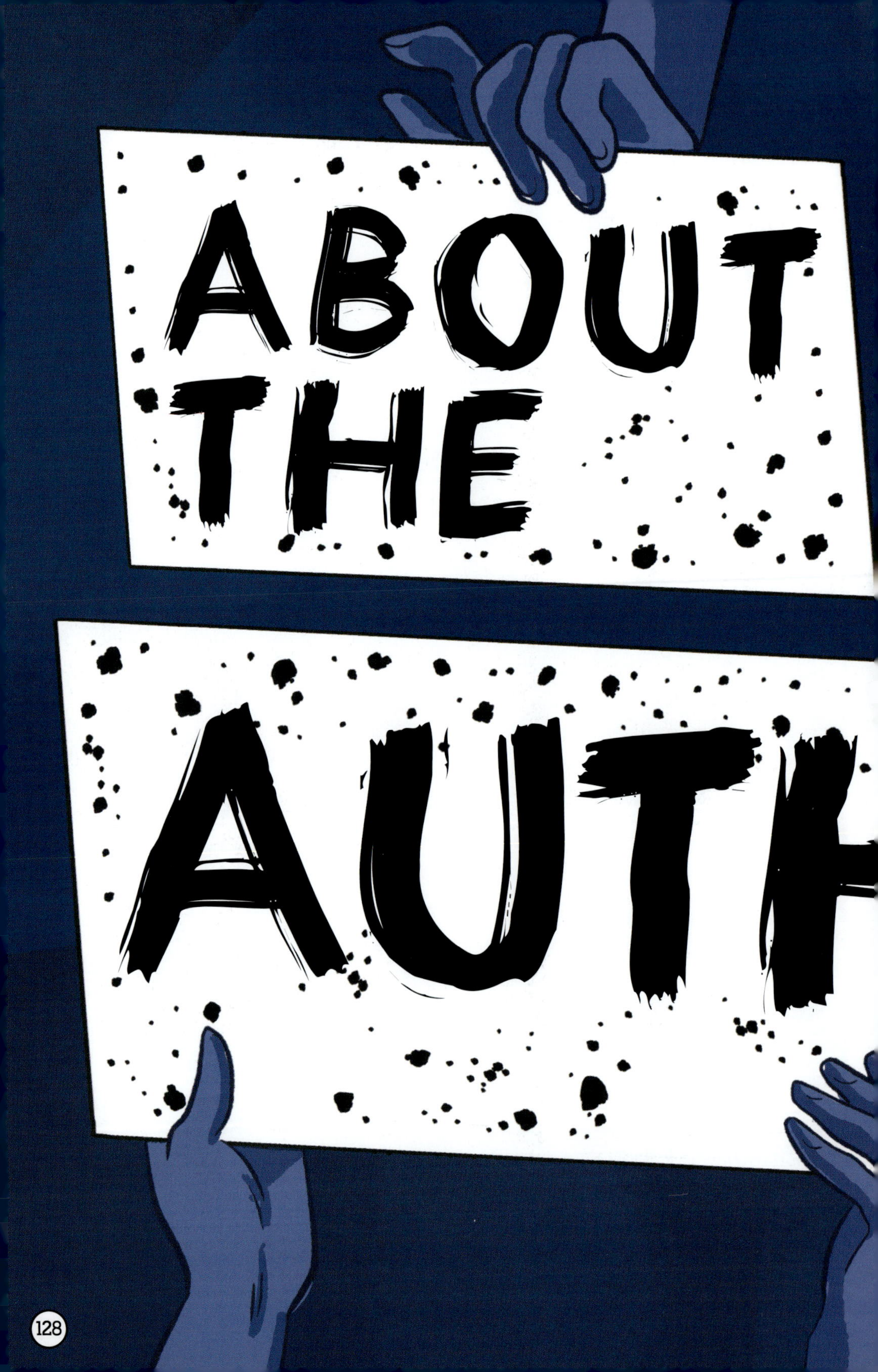
ABOUT THE
AUTH

ADA JUSIC

Ada Jusic is a Bosnian artist and animator. She was born in Sarajevo and came to the UK aged four as a refugee.

Art and creativity were how she made sense of her story and identity. Now she works to help others do the same - through thought-provoking animation and illustration.

Ada also paints murals and enjoys working with young people to teach them creative skills and is passionate about advocating for young people to have better access to the arts.

She lives in London with her husband, son and two cats.

RAMSEY HASSAN

Ramsey Hassan is a London based writer and illustrator who has worked in comics (as RAMZEE), animation and theatre. He was nominated for a British Comic Award in 2016 and won the Second Text Prize in Fab Prize 2017. Ramsey likes to tell fun and heart-warming stories about characters from backgrounds that are rarely depicted.

MARIE BAMYANI

Marie Bamyani left Afghanistan in 2021 during the Fall of Kabul and is now based in Germany. Marie is a former psychologist turned author. As an Afghan woman, Marie uses her voice as an author to shine a light on women's experiences in Afghanistan under Taliban rule and to share the real-life experience of refugees.

SONYA ZHURENKO

Sonya Zhurenko fled her home country of Ukraine when the conflict between Ukraine and Russia started in 2022. She now lives with her family in Italy. Sonya was fifteen years old when writing about her experiences as a refugee.

NADINE KAADAN

Nadine Kaadan is an award-winning children's book author and illustrator from Syria now living in London. She is published in several countries and languages and her mission is to champion empowered and inclusive representation in children's books so that every child can see themselves in a story.

Nadine's work with young refugees in reducing the impact of post-conflict trauma has captured the attention of CNN and the BBC, and both have broadcast special features on her books 'Tomorrow' and 'The Jasmine Sneeze'. She has been nominated for a Kate Greenaway Medal, and is the 2019 winner of the Arab British Centre Award for Culture. Nadine was selected as one of The BBC 100 Women 2020's 'most influential and inspiring women', and was featured on their BBC 100 Women masterclass. In 2021, Nadine was commissioned by The Story Museum to be the writer of Amal Meets Alice, a procession event in Oxford that gathered over 100 performers with 8,000 people joining on the day.

Her latest book, 'The Kind Activity Book', illustrated by Nadine and Axel Scheffler – illustrator of the Gruffalo – is published by Scholastic and part of its proceeds will be donated to The Three Peas – a charity NGO that supports Syrian refugees.

GLOSSARY

ABDICATE – When a king or queen gives up their right to be a monarch.

ALLIES OR ALLIED POWERS – The countries that had formed an agreement to fight the Axis powers during the Second World War. The major Allied countries were Great Britain, the United States and the Soviet Union.

AL-QAEDA – An extremist Islamic organization who want to rule the Muslim countries in the east. They often use violence to attack other countries.

ANNEXING – Usually done after military occupation, annexation is when one country forcibly takes a part of another's territory.

ARCHAEOLOGY – The study of ancient and recent history, through the analysis of artefacts and other physical remains, such as the ruins of ancient cities.

ASSASSINATION – The murder of an important person by a surprise attack, usually for a political or religious reasons.

ASYLUM – Protection granted to a person by a country to a person who has left their home country because they have experienced persecution or human rights violations.

AXIS POWERS – Countries allied with Germany during WW2, including Italy and Japan.

CENTRAL POWERS – The opposing parties during WW1. The Central Powers was an alliance made up of Germany, Austria-Hungary, the Ottoman Empire and Bulgaria.

CHADARI – A garment which fully covers the face and body, worn by women.

CIVIL WAR – A war fought among opposing groups of people within the same country.

CITY STATE – An independent and self-governed city and its surrounding area.

COLONY – A place under the political control of another country.

COMMUNISM – A political belief that wealth and ownership of property should be shared by everyone in a society.

COUP – A sudden and usually violent attempt to seize power from an existing government.

CRUSADES, THE – A series of religious wars during the eleventh to thirteenth centuries, in which Christian knights tried to seize control of Jerusalem which was then under Muslim rule.

DICTATOR – A person who rules a country by themselves, and has no restriction on their power.

DISPLACED – A person who is forced to leave their home country because of a war or natural disaster.

DYNASTY – A series of rulers from successive generation of one family.

EID – A religious festival that occurs twice a year. Eid-ul-Adha is celebrated after Hajj. Eid-ul-Fitr takes place the day after the last fast of Ramadan.

EMPIRE – A collection of lands and territories led by one ruler or government.

FIRST WORLD WAR – A global conflict taking place between 1914–1918, fought in Europe and many other countries in Africa, Asia and the Middle East.

GENOCIDE – The deliberate killing of a large number of people that belong to a certain ethnic, religious or political group.

GOVERNMENT – A group of people with the authority to rule a country.

HAZARA – An ethnic group of people from Afghanistan.

HIJAB – A garment that covers the head and is worn by some Muslim women.

IMMIGRANT – A person who moves to and permanently lives in a foreign country.

LABOUR CAMPS – Prisons where the inmates are forced to do hard labour.

MONARCHY – A type of government which recognizes a king or queen as head of state, even though they may not hold any political power.

PRESIDENT – The head of an elected government.

PROTECTORATE – A country that is controlled and protected by another more powerful state.

REBELLION – Opposition to authority.

REFERENDUM – A general vote on a specific political issue.

REFUGEE – A person who has been forced to leave their home country because of war or a natural disaster.

SCRAMBLE FOR AFRICA – Between 1881 and 1914, European powers invaded, divided and colonized Africa.

SECOND WORLD WAR – A global conflict between two groups of countries, the Allies and the Axis Powers between 1939 - 1945.

SERFS – A labourer who would work on a particular person's land and could not leave without their permission. If the land was sold, the serf was sold with it.

SHARIA LAWS – The religious laws of Islam.

SHIA – A sect of Islam.

SLAVE – A person who is held and forced to work against their will and is considered the property of another.

SOCIALISM – The belief that a government should be able to control the economy to help spread wealth evenly across everyone in a society.

SOVIET UNION – Union of Soviet Social Republics or the Soviet Union for short, a communist state including Russia and other countries.

TRIBE – A group of people who live together and share the same language, culture or ancestors.

UPRISING – An act of rebellion against a government.

INDEX